COLUMBIA POETRY REVIEW

Columbia College/Chicago

Spring 1992

Columbia Poetry Review is published in the spring of each year by the English Department of Columbia College, 600 South Michigan Avenue, Chicago, Illinois 60605. Submissions are encouraged and should be sent to the above address. Subscriptions and sample copies are available at $6.00 an issue.

Grateful acknowledgement is made to Dr. Philip Klukoff, Chairman of the English Department; Dr. Sam Floyd, Academic Vice-President; Lya Rosenblum, Dean of Graduate Studies; Bert Gall, Administrative Vice-President; and Mike Alexandroff, President of Columbia College.

The cover photograph is by John Mulvany.

Student Editors:

John Boyer
Carolyn Koo
Barbara Slaga

Faculty Advisor:

Paul Hoover

CONTENTS

Columbia Poetry Review

CHARLES SIMIC

CAGED FORTUNETELLER

Sleeplessness, you're like a pawnshop
Open late
On a street of failing businesses.
The owner plays a flute,
And it's like night birds calling
In a city where there are no birds.

There's a painting over the cash register:
Of a stiff Quaker couple dressed in black.
They each hold a cat under their arm.
One is a tiger, the other is Siamese.
The eyes are closed because it's very late,
And because cats see better with eyes closed.

The pawnshop owner has an electric fortuneteller
In a glass cage.
Now he plugs her in and turns the other lights off.
"O foolish fellow," says she,
"If you can find your way, please hurry to me,
I'll even take out my breasts at the door
To light your way in the dark."

The street is shadowy and so is the sky.
We could be meeting Jacob and the angel.
We could be meeting our sleeplessness,
And the nun who carries morphine to the dying,
The black nun in soft, furry slippers.

1

CAROLINE KNOX

TONKA

On the broad broadloom
a child impels a large Tonka;
it's a brownish truck,
a UPS Tonka. "How's
Mac?" "Good," he says. (He *is* Mac.)

MacArthur said, "I
shall return." Harry Truman
said, "You bet you shall."
When Harry delivered this,
his tool was rage, not the tank.

(Bess said, "I *won't* tell
him to say 'fertilizer';
it's taken me all
of these twenty-five years, sir,
to get him to say 'manure.' ")

So MacArthur retraced
the track back to the redoubt,
who had once been heard
to say elsewhere, "Lafayette,
we are here," in another

context, and that chief
was not the Cincinnatus
de nos jours.

        His con-
stituents said, "Give 'em hell,
Harry," and so Harry did,
if you'd please excuse
his French. It was Eisenhower,
it was Ike, as I
recall, who put "under God" in
the Pledge of Allegiance, though.

I like Ike OK.
He said that the DAR
could not inhibit
Marian Anderson's song
in their frosty bailiwick.

Yours truly and intrusive-
ly avers that all
this stuff is over the head
of the young Mac met
back in stanza one, but yet

time may provide that
with diligence said Mac may
select role models
for art and/or commerce high
as any Motown icon.

CONVERSATIONS AVEC MARCEAU

Oh, Hatshepsut, it is your turn to play
senet with young Horus here and Thoth.
Where are the socks? They are in the crisper.

You hold in your hand the proxy of our view:
      the group is the text
      at the Colorado School of Mimes.
Our friends are such formidable co-religionists
they have a chasuble on the grand piano
and carpeting that doubles as furniture—
you wear snowshoes, unless you want to go to sleep.

My "spouse" is of the Druid faith;
when I want his advice, I'll ask for it,
as cassettes about metaphysics snap into your brain
      when you are full of love
      like light into the public library.

SUSAN WHEELER

FORECAST FOR A PRACTICAL SOLUTION

The man carries several watercolors across the street.
Their mats are bound, and the backings
        are taped idiosyncratically.
He did these watercolors at a time when his friend irked.

The man pretends now he lives in Gdansk.
He passes the coffeeshop where he sat with
        the woman under warrant
        for employing homeworkers.
Its windows are soaped.

A child shouts *Detdetdetda exCUSE me.*
She has washed all the dishes and put them
        in the drain
and now she wheels on the steps.

He passes the park where a man
        after a long walk pulled at
        his thumb as he talked
just as though he were beating off.

A family stops in the sunset—
he leans on his feet—
he fills a hole the dog dug.

The dog, dazzled by a light which falls but on him,
        drenched in the moving stands,
illumines sod, a blazoned mutt.

The man feels a pinch beneath
        his fly as he walks.
Trash wire, just emptied, rolls on its rim.

The man passes the building where the girl sobbed
        when she spoke about the closet.
There is a sheriff's notice in the southeast window.

He could have walked backward but he didn't.
The scenery is accidental.
The sequence he wishes were accidental.
It was almost a bagpipe he could hear from far off.

He is shivering.
A firefly batters his shoulder and whirrs again away.

in memorium, Bill Gwin, 1947-1990

LIVING WITH APPEARANCES

On the lake the flecked boats weave
And meet and wend away, rebuffed.
This tensifying palls the
Tended office of the dean,
Whose eyes fix on the aqua sky,
Rake the blue, careen.

What did we lose on these the books
That reason won't retrieve?
Several clouds collide upon the point,
And then several colleagues leave.

JOHN TRANTER

AURORA

I love the flush of the Reached Zenith,
but there's also a swerve to remember—
the junior glow, the teen fracas, drifting
among skittish louts and kids
malingering behind the snack frames—
siblings hiding in a heap of theology, that
locker. Jab and gargle, Drain-Brain,
make a zig-zag run for the future!
Patrol—window choked with tourists—
that lolls past the floral clock,
and idles by the turkey-talkers
on the breakwater—where else?
The cruise grumblers, called "Jumbo"
and "Drop-Kick," moon; in a back paddock
the starlight jalopy dump breeds dreams.
Dumb in the pokey this small town admits it is,
the sleepers wander in the fields of childhood;
ah, bright graduation: it's the
turncoat kid giving the farm away
for Sin City, burning the vacant role

Just as you're strutting in the avenue vocal with juveniles, it forms a dreadful
pattern—don't you merit a hi after all those cycles? And time avenging, in
the village pub a line-up of slender singles groggy in the purple light, the
hoon range brute drudge-drivers, why, automatic Country & Western, this
is the monochrome fifties your heart a banging pump, the old bus grinding
gears pulling out in rain-swept daybreak, grey paint smeared and winter
overcoat decorum exit our hope gap bye-bye lacklustre muddy chief route
abyss

CUBANS

Under the fog-lights, weaving from
one side of the highway to the other,
the wheel damp and slippery in your hands,
the sound of water in the gutters then
        splashing on concrete,
tyres on a wet surface back and
        forth across the courtyard
circling and reversing in the storm,
and the knock and scratch of wipers
left-right, left-right. Past Korea-Town—
a thousand neon signs "only Asians can read"—
then New Havana and acres of
oil derricks. A police car stranded
belly across the gutter at an angle,
five young men spreadeagled
against a chain-link fence,
three cops with guns out, screaming.
White lettering with a green outline,
lit from behind, spelling out
a curse and a remedy at the same time

She turns over and the sagging mattress moves, making a chinking sound beneath the bed—wine bottles clink, a suggestion for music—one tone, two tones—dull marimba. Moving slowly under the lamplight someone breaks a piece of bread in half, and smears it with sweet yellow oil from a tin. The pen running out of ink. "CAR TIRES IN THE RAIN" scratched on a phone message pad with a ball-point pen, almost out of ink, then scrawled with a burnt match-stick. Outside it's still raining, still pouring down.

CAMBRIDGE COUPLES

Nix vexation, nitwit crazy
unfeigned ketch boundary
torrent prevailing the tack
tally minus the heyday netting
counterfeits ancient numerals,
better than dud coins, master.
The academic guardian channels
terminate titanic critique spouse
she voodoos and sayonara
crack-up each ashen
sparkle hug wasted,
the witness hopes a pliable
trace of render aft rapture
racked up by raft,
pout alongside yours, blow
perfectly the drift into
your lip synch you
implore that tally
henceforth, precious
shadowy lens

Recently graduated couples (four sensitive people) wander down a twilight tow-path (item: Greek myths) share a glow—they're 'it' this year, nouveau art flash, more riveting than the invention of a new Chinese dish, wire urgent by-line/Boston/Friday reads "revulsion from the true avant-garde cutting edge boiling up from far side Pacific Rim, snapshot wet flash synch bleach over sand, up the beach, wreckage and wrack flooding Cambridge, 1936"; end" their wistful dreams (share reflective cigarette) but that's good too—"Golly, Jill, I'm drenched!"—fresh meat for the grinder, clouds blurring the hills promise rain

CHARLES BERNSTEIN

THE IRON RING AND THE ECSTASY

I never met a man I liked
Nor woman who liked me
But Love's not grace it's Song
& Life's not long it's Story

The Frontier's not too Far they say
But hardly a boat will go the Way
Once there was a Ferry though
No bridge spans half the Bay

Let's make Amends & say we're friends
I Know that friends don't Lie
Let's take a trip to Alabaster Tip
& say that we have Tried

No boat to sail, no plane to fly
No feet to walk or run
Still where there's Fashion hope remains
Hope that does not Hide

THE DOG IS DEAD

A friend of mine named Rudy Loop
Says time's the noblest thing
I think I know better when I say
I prefer soup to stew

The sandpiper knows not where to nest
A bee can find no bone
The baby never stops crying
But I must have my lunch

BARBARA CAMPBELL

THE IRISH BIRTH

1. before

O virgin of virgins, my mother I found
you flat and damp and muddied O sullen
mother in the gutter, we are this: Irish
Permanent and 4 p.m. We are nothing.
On bright days my hands wrap
your thumb and I walk all knock-
kneed long Jesus feet. A corn
god. At night I fly
to you knitting needles broken
ankles. One big stick. Mother,
the air is carnage, and my crown
digging your cheek home under

and under a husband trying
to sleep or not.

2. the miracle

Mother, the seats are filled
with men and their fingers. My blood
and time are strange
as the rain & monkeys running
through an Irish town. Here
in the hay with my hair
spread out having wrapped the pink
sheets, I watch the sheep
cry, all the animals, all this
religion. My mind is wrong.
I will plug myself with sons, a choir of
sons and semen and beeswax. I know what

sends people out into the streets: the cups
and nothing—the trick of it.

HOLIDAY WITH SMALL MAN & VINEYARD

Sing me the pull
and push, a Spanish
song, this untouched
boat of us. At home
we spoke toads
of notes and bars
rested. Splitgut frog, god-
head of song slicked
open at night under
tire and oar and opened
bourbon. *I've never had*
bourbon. Sing
and drink it short;
we have just three
days. Draw me
up like a line of fish—
scrawny, salty, relieved of my
breathing. The boat
is open, is orange and baking
through the day, its little
neck the map home. Draw
me a map
of all the little
houses and thick black
phone line right
down to my neck and
cording. Draw all
my veins, the beach of
my mouth, our
bed and knitted
blanket.

DAVE MEAD

POEM ON WINTER GLASS

should i drink tonight
  'til bones tear callus and
    blue? 'til every reaction's
      peanut-dumb, sold for quarters
        like flags, boners and religion
          by

proxy? from where i lie
  nothing is done for a browning
    lawn's cancer, for the dogbane's
      inability to ply my buckteeth and
        lust, nothing 'til i dread the sense
          of

midnight sighs, a duck-
  billed cap, the tremble
    of rubies in the small of
      her back. (what i really love
        is catching melissa's scent, mist-
          wet

on a knuckle hair, in
  the crook of an arm, and
    when she mumbles "jesus"
      in her sleep, i hear the
        tri-cornered concrete out-
          side

on lincoln that shimmers,
  fraying rain.) but when you're
    twentytwo and damp moonlight crimps
      the blinds, shitting the hollow floor
        where you once lay a hat, you value the
          strength

in wallframes, a sinking fast-
  ball, your father's forearms, and
    when you finally surface, focused but
      starving, with skin of blight that scabs
        only in mending its fury, you open a wrist
        and

let that
  rust limp
    and pool.

OUR SISTERS

(Dear girl with the pursed lips who fell asleep,
with her head tossed back, four or five seats in
front of me, on the train last night:

innocent.
like a church at dawn,
any woman talking
    behind
your back'd
feel like she'd just
spent Christmas Eve
in a porn shop.............and
(forgive me, I ramble)
drunken men
in groups of ten'd
see you
working a crossword puzzle
on a midnight train
and they'd point
to you
with crude winks
and nudges
(secretly seeing you as
one of those gasoline rainbows
in a puddle of melted snow
on their driveway that
they walk around instead
of through), knowing
that cumming and
watching children surfacing,
laughing, after jumping into
a pile of leaves
would only feel half as good,
realizing that,
if you wanted,
any one of them'd
go home with you
to wait in your yard,
with snow melting in their hair,
until your bedroom

17

light
sank
safely
out.............and
I,
if you said,
"I need
you, too,"
would let you lead—
anywhere. And every time you'd
fall asleep
I'd drop dried
rose petals
onto your pursed
lips.)

BARBARA SLAGA

DUCHESS IN A SMALL TOWN

She had mirrors in her hair
and beyond the light of glass
and rings, she dreamed of
boulevards with meaning
that lead to distant dead ends.
The streets that force you
to crawl over a fence or bush,
lifting your skirt to
get through to the sea
and its nameless face.

She sat on a rock
and mimicked the townspeople,
waiting for mid-season
to melt the apples to the ground.
Her lover sits on the side
contemplating better use
of their time.
The town is bent
and she glimpses the leaf train
and the branch bed inside her sleeper,
the tender alignment of sea and hive.
She lives there
within centuries of old lace
crocheted in silk.

Sitting still
he mentions a lone spiral
that shows what is and why
and he being a friend,
a cloud, a clown
told her to back off
take off her shoes
and barter with the coin collector.
Figure on dying twice
small and weightless
to music that holds your breath.

19

MOODS IN AN ATTIC

Wood like a tomb of surprises
blatantly telling me where I am.
Creaking its oak panels
in a panic of rooms.

Falling in a crowd.
Making faces behind the mirror
you'll never see.
Tired of limping.
You take in all the
wretched coldness and
you're gone.

The body knows
more than the mind.
Tap the shoulder and
everything turns.
Bending the rules and letting
premonitions take a seat.

She called me by so many names
that I recognize.
Swarms of plays read out loud
            drop,
breaking ice on the bookshelves.
No candles, no lights,
just eyes in the mood room.
Organ music changing
your sensibilities to dirt.

Dark dots pressed on a dress.
Every house has an angry one of these—
knowing wood kept still.
They talk in the hours you can't count.
Anchoring the tendency to leave.

LIVING TOGETHER

Silent air in a dish
scooped in a silent drink.
Not boring or surreal,
just edible
like love, like feeling
down where it all begins.
An anxious melody.
All the sound the room
collects and passes out.

Sex is good.
It's like air and room
bordering together,
comforting each with
its existence.

The tale:
Charlie gave Pam a ruby
and the ruby caved in
and became roses
and the roses ran away
through every door . . .

and it's all predictable
red things, I mean.
Any color that can be defined.
The sound of air.
The room that blinds itself
is worth talking about.

I met you in a room
neat and dusted.
Trying to talk itself
out of safety.
Trying to climb each corner.
Wondering what the ceiling
feels like.
Aging the hardwood floors with
the soles of our feet.

ANGELA JACKSON

JOYCE SAYS

Joyce says the man just ain't right.
He got some kinda problem hid outta sight.
And it's making itself known in his peculiar behavior.
O, he present hisself real good first like a saint or savior.
But then the seams start showin
And you be knowin
He tryin to cover up what keep kickin the covers off.

Maybe it stem for a deprived childhood.
Maybe he'd be better if itta would.
Maybe he were ugly and his mama dress him funny.
Maybe everything psychological grow from lack of money.
Joyce says the man just ain't right.
Anyway a wishbone probably got a bonehead jaws tight.
Probably like to ride cows/ made up gapped like that.
Probably got ashy legs crusty feet and go to sleep in he hat.
Joyce says you sure you wanna be involved with a individual
who still got the travelling residual
in he physique?

MY DREAM BO

I am a real character laughing in a cartoon.
In no room for nightmare, tortuous and grim.
My heart pumps up with the dream of him.
I am crazy, sanely crazy as a loon.

Now sorcerous scenarios, quickening winding roads
for magic,
comic,
sexually explicit.

This limber peace eases by lame logic.
It passes all understanding:

O! Now this man's body is a wishbone
in blue overalls.
His long, long legs a long blue bow.
Anatomically a wonder.
O!
I wonder how I'll love him
when light is light or dim.
But I do.
When new air and sky rush through
him. I can see blue bent tender around blue.
O!
The thing that connects him to me, must come
out of his throat like a song.

like
a song.

MOMENT

Each moment is infinite and complete.

After you get up to go and I can think of no more reasons
for you to stay that I can say without making it all too plain
more plain than what is safe later to look at after we have both
had our way with each other and we don't know yet where to go
with each other or even if we want to, we stand out in front
of the house like proper would-be lovers courting
in an earlier century.
I start staring up at the stars because I want to see a falling star,
and you follow because you have far more experience at star-gazing
than I. You are quick and see two, but I see none,
only the after-effect of stars in the vicinity of the falling who talk
in coded light after the one goes down, "Yonder he goes; yonder she runs."
That is what I know they say, but you say this is not so
I only think it is
and I say it is so and how do you know
and you say maybe so.
Then you tell me about light, how old it is and how new, how you first
saw time while you sat close by a river that bent; it was then and
it was now is now and it was easier for you to live after that
or was it before
you know it now.
I do too. You have always been standing under this sky with me.
I have always been here somewhere near you.
When you bend down and I arch up, my breasts ending
like starpoints pushing against you,
we make a bow for a moment. You turn your mouth to my cheek and say,
"You are beautiful." Then you kiss me.
I look over my shoulder at all those stars and see you.
"You're beautiful."
Now I say the stars that fall are falling in love.
And what do you say then?

DAVID BRESKIN

DOCUMENTARY

Blue cranes among kudu,
the sand grouse captured
by terrapin teeth, a black
crane standing on the nose
of a rhino, pecking at the
bright red gash where the
horn's been ripped off in
a battle for sex.

Rubber bustier, high heels
tweek the unpainted ass, rouge
nipples plus Angel Cordero's
riding crop is the contrasty
mise en scene, the Malibu beach
house, rented by the hour to
feed the frenzy of Hitchcock
sharks, Peckinpah bloody lips,
parted, licky teeth.

Ostrich by zebra by springbok,
the banded mongeese rile warthogs
and blacksmith plovers, while
the snorkeling python, nostrils
hidden in the water weed, goes at
the Egyptian goose, which flies,
but the red-billed coot is not
so lucky. Flamingoes are rarely
seen with wildebeest.

Lace teddy, police nightstick,
Uma Thurmanish, soft focus,
flexible muted cries on formica,
local three piece suit unzipped,
certain kinds of fellas, squeezing,

those two dimples above her hind
quarters, smiling purse certainly
exchange of bills.

Avocet sweep the cloudy water
with bills for small change of
crustaceans. Another Kennedy
drives off another bridge.
The jackal makes everyone
at the water hole slightly
apprehensive. Hot tubs are
traditional for this kind of
shot, where she's on top.
Everyone is making a living.

SEMTEX / PA 103

in memory of David Dornstein (1962-1989)

10. My mother is weeping over my grave.
   She places a pink rose petal on my name.
   She kisses my name.
   The petal sticks to her lips for an instant.
   She washes the stone and the stone darkens.
   I see the stupidity of everything.

9. Tonight, on television, red water cascades from a fountain's
      crying mouth.
   Snow geese fly in circles above the site of the crash.
   Elvis makes good as a stock-car driver.

8. The point is to get from one place to another.
   All our lives, that's it.
   Squiggly tubes and tissue, ambitions, trivia, lunch boxes,
      clothing, desires, underwear, misunderstandings, all
      from one place to another.

7. I was a student of history.
   I see now even the stupidity of history.
   A revolution describes a perfect circle.
   Man is born free but everywhere is in chain stores.
   Those that don't know their fathers are condemned to be them.

6. I am now a student of SEMTEX.
   It has taught me everything again, in a brand new way.
   I bathe in SEMTEX, filling my bathtub with it, christening the
      hard yellow plastic rubber ducks of childhood.
   I eat SEMTEX, which is surprisingly tasty, especially with
      raspberries in the morning.
   SEMTEX is my pillow when I'm weary, my drink when I'm thirsty.
   It's my mail at noon and my love at night.
   Goodnight.

5. When I got to Scotland, the air was damp and cold, the men
      busy with short-waves.
   I must say the investigators treated us very, very well.
   You'll get no complaints from me.

27

The entire bunch was first-rate, it was.
It was much worse for them than it was for us.
(Some of us still had shallowy breath, pulsing.)
The looks on their faces.

4. On Broadway at midnight, the bus driver exhales his last fare.
   He darkens his destination sign and nails pedal to floor.
   He wants to fly home.
   He thinks about his wife's fine fingernails in bed.
   He hasn't given me a thought.
   I'm not saying I'm hurt, but.

3. The florist's flowers bleed.
   The drunkard's ulcers bleed.
   The balance sheet bleeds.
   The boxer bleeds.
   The tape bleeds.
   The paint bleeds.
   The woman, she bleeds, baby.

2. Take one dumb horse's life, for instance.
   Standing so smooth and easy in the field, waiting for the stud,
       nibbling at Kentucky bluegrass under soft skies.
   Why is she not flying to battle, head erect and ears up?
   Why is she not under the Conquistador?
   The Confederate?
   The Roman?

1. We are all born dead.
   The early morning edition is dumped off the truck and swung
       onto the stand with the sad promise of tomorrow's head.
   A certain amount of living is done, somewhere between sea turtle
       and blue-footed booby.
   The woman inside the bank feeds the machines.
   The door of the past swings in, not out.
   My mother can't sleep, and she walks downstairs, and she turns on
       the set, and she takes her pill and she wets herself.

0.

LOST AISLE OF DOGS (SHOPPING SAFEWAY)

for Blake Hallanan

Kill only things you understand, all else
let go. The maid spanks her lord like clockwork.
Bring me the sweat of Scottie Pippen, bankers
and brokers, meter maids. Analize skin
for it's content of wind. Excuse me, while
I kiss the skull. Birthing cows twitch like fish
on neon flies, the eddy circling backwards.
The kayak drills your stomach with its fist,
inside-out Eskimo rolls the Klondike
caper. Eastern gods of yen buy Hawaii
not to mention Manhattan Kansas. Bulked
on steroids, yakuzas finger victims. Go slow.

Clip coupons, T-bills dogshit in rising
interest rate scenario but milkbones still
milkbones. Breath better, coat glowing, mind
sharp. The checkout girl has VPL and bags
under her armpits. Muzak makes the checks
go down like Darvon. Sting by strings, waltzing.

I'm no Martha, I'm no Vandella. Breast
tissue does not solve the problem. Pith helmuts
dangle over dop kits, raised pleasure
dots packing. Don't jump to delusions here.
The countryside of ancient Rome combines
aqueducts with plastic pails, blue cranes, brown
flats: an eight-by-ten eye is big enough to
squeeze it. I'm falling apart here is what
Dustin says in the midnight hour, dobies
sniffing heels. Never help a victim. Go
seek help, wine or gun. A bullet in the nose
beats a quail in the bush, red foxes leaping.

NATALIE KENVIN

SKIN

What does he want?
He loves the dank salt in the crook of
My neck.
He parts me, my lips soft and nacreous.
Is this the central place,
The plumb line of the body?
Is this where the dark ladder of impulse
Reaches?
I will cry among nettles
Because of the deception
Of the body's want.
A bond, a knot, a balancing
Of bone and grievance in an equilibrium
So sickness and grief become a knot
To be undone.
There is a refusal to cry,
To end as decomposing leaves
Or the tiny bits of birds' bones
In the droppings of a fox.

BEATING

My father knows only that
There is a woman's humid readiness
About my mother,
Her hair messy, lying in ringlets
That smell of copper.
Now she is going to get it,
He says.
He strikes her once and she falls
Back from the medicinal skid
Of his calloused right hand.
Now he is balancing on top of
Her fallen body with his left leg,
His right suspended in the air
Like one might balance on a log.
She says "Don't."
For a moment they are caught here
In the spit of craziness.
He lets her up.
They walk to the kitchen.
They sit at the table
In a convalescent indolence,
A queer lassitude.
He pours a curl of cream into her tea,
Turning it a tarnished color.
She drinks, hooking her fingers
Around the cup.
He eats a small cracker.
I stare at them.
They are shameless
And in a great solitude.

CONNIE DEANOVICH

KISSING THE FEET OF TALENT

Katharine Hepburn
you throne
that throws me
riverside
like a runaway
Miss Energy
swimming through mud
to see Roosevelt
of course
it started
with a helicopter
unable
to land
Every sunrise
rebirths you
romantic bridges
shape Sunday into
the luggage bought
the genius unmarried
Unmarried?!?
Nefertiti photographs eyes
as rivers
braids
gold boullion
important in the past
like a handshake
like a gowned god
borrowed from the attic

Spencer Tracy
you rubdown
that breathes me
athletic
olympically weird and
chlorined hair
Spot the swimmers in study hall

and next day Alex dead
on the train tracks
in the body bags
coffin cradled
and cried for by school intercom
touch the boy become a man
with problems pricking
him a face
Pollock
use an ice skate across that picture
the picture that makes
good times seem better
a bigger wedding cake
and firmer chastity

BEAUTIFUL BEAUTY PARLOR

I have a curtain drawn over the mirror
fuschia
depicting a tale
me
as a normal knight
only straddling a motorcycle
gnawing a cantaloupe

Didn't there used to be mini TVs
clamped to beauty shop chair arms
to stare into?

The tale begins to traipse through time

love affair
to
pure gray hair
the baby losing its milk teeth

It's so boring to be fussed over AND
make conversation: Hawaiian elopement,
what pink can do for you

I say
look good as a boy
and now I'm the strange one
maybe lice or something soft on my scalp

But they make you be wet in the window,
smother you with cigarette ash and call it
industrial. It's all about looks. And what
I want's intangible behavior, surplus energy.

GENERIC TEENAGER

Comes with changeable ponytail
and a time machine

with one boy
or another

or a girl comes with her mother
to model her into Miss Universe

the blue eyes of smiling Texas
she gives

like
one shit

dinosaurs lived there before her
she thinks dinosaurs are the

invention of the whole world—unreal,
conjured, masculine, and

no way did some of them not eat meat
her teeth, like theirs, are specimens

her bones as agile
as theirs really were

when she does the Cake Walk
across the vast plain of the athletic field

she trips the time machine
and we thank her for it

PAUL HOOVER

PLEASURE

It is said that the pleasure of language
is its purity of intention, the will
to jettison will. Pleasure in eating a peach
and pleasure in watching the mess. As we approach

the academic year, I thought it apropos
to mention the pleasure of thinking,
of remembering having thought.
Like the blue beyond the door, the light

leans strangely here, as if in pleasure's head.
Or to put it the other way, repeating the actions
of water succumbs to sponge this down.
I'm mixing sentences here. Yet inside *yet,*

the truly depraved rave in the sweat
I made at last retreat. You find this beautiful.
Thanks for your kind attention. (Alms for the real,
the bells pealed, reality for the dead.)

Or in the opposing instance a package says,
"This free gift of flowers (Forget-Me-Nots)
can only fund a disease with the help
of those like you. Sow when danger of frost

is past, covering seeds 1/8 inch deep."
A melancholy pleasure is pleasure nevertheless.
In the mind it's like a meadow or rather
a visual field so pleasantly distracting

it looks like something to eat. The pointillist
points depart from their intentions,
which makes them moments of pleasure.
Anxieties and frets pull themselves

to the window where they shake like violets,
and there you are, attempting happiness
with a word like "chalk" in your mouth,
wanting love without the hunger.

There's no pleasure in that.
So you get sleepy a lot and lie here
watching the snow as it covers your face
and softens each weld like an edge.

It feels like pleasure but acts like pain
and happened at the urge of language,
which wants what it wants when it wants it
once it decides on an object of pleasure.

THE SAME DIFFERENCE

This is where things stand at the moment.
The need to express oneself
and not reveal too much
of what one really ought to be feeling
creates a tone of mandarin calm
reminiscent of clouds, the great cumulus galleons
that verge upon bad taste.
But soon everything declines to farce,
banal pratfalls, newspapers landing in bushes
where the damp householder has to scramble for them.
One is a kind of inflation, precise to the degree
that language is like clouds;
the other deflates to what we know is true.
Comic and democratic, it seems embarrassed there.
This morning, I saw a bird
land on the back of a bird
fashioned from blue concrete,
the "beauty" of the moment had more to do with blue
than with the living bird, but on the whole
the urge to transcendence keeps us alive.
We want to balloon through the atmosphere
with blue wings at our backs.
Then again, as I left the movie early,
I thought: life is like the movies,
a thousand frozen moments comprising a single action,
while death is a simple photograph
evoking carnival smoke, pastness you carry with you.
You balance light and shade
with a minimal tone of importance,
in the way a suicide note
can never be less than earnest.
But the metaphor of the note
can overwhelm the original thought,
which had to do with sitting there,
trying to resolve your complex feelings
of grandeur. Well, even grandeur
must be imagined. Between the blue concrete
and a blurred photograph of leaves
lies something precise but inexact
like the look of specific vagueness

one sees on the secretly blessed.
It's all part of an abstract picture:
scenes from childhood shaken in a glass,
snow falls on the little town
where the train is about to leave,
having arrived six years ago.
If you hold it to the light,
you can see your face wrap it like a world.

JAMES McMANUS

FROM GREAT AMERICA

Bring all your money when you come
to Great America. Entire
sunburned families do. Single moms
and dads with their kids for

the weekend, visitation rights
for perhaps all of August;

grammar school girls with one strap
of their overalls dangling down
to their coltish and intricate kneecaps;

sneering, tattooed, earringed teenagers
with miniscule pimples and mustaches,
real jerkoffs, in heavy metal polyester
T-shirts: Anthrax, Motorhead, U.S.,

G 'N' R, Husker Du, Poison, the same bad Rod
Stewart-Farah Fawcett hairdo
to a man as their fidgety dates; clearly proud

devotees of Rich Falk Basketball Camp and Zora Neale
Hurston, the White Sox, the Pogues, Jane's Addiction; the usual

well-behaved, plainly groomed and clothed Asians . . .

Suddenly this gorgeous, unmated
Latina in one-ply white Dago
T with the dewy, finely delineated
backs of her knees revealed under slow

grind and spark of blue skirt
comes lowriding by *and then gone!*
as we're herded through tubular aluminum mazes in tight
longitudinal zigzag, penned in

36 rows going one way
37 rows in the other

configured in-
geniously so that one

only rarely simply
stands there and waits, every

last person in their fleshly summer glory: no-tan
lines, cellulite, weightlifter triceps and squints, armpit hair, noshing

cheesedogs, powder blue cotton candy, burritos, icecream
novelties, Pizza Luigi, soft pretzels, all of us trudging along

for fifty-five minutes for sixty or seventy seconds
on Splashwater Falls, Ameri-Go-Round, Rolling Thunder, the Demon . . .

In line for the Eagle I spot Samuel Beckett's gulls'
eyes glaring out from the chest of a slackly buxom Ms.

I'm im-
pressed. Because upon snatching a brief *hmm*

surruptitious but closer inspection, it's the Sucking Stones
passage from the Tetralogy *distributed them equally between*

my four above her poor breasts. The front side of one
leg of her kneelength shorts is red. The front

of the other leg's black and features a furrow-browed
snorting red bull with white red-tipped horns. The pattern's reversed

on the back of the shorts, except there's no logo to break up the line
of her backside, *de dum* . . . The American

Eagle's an old-fashioned wooden double roller-coaster,
an abstracted white boa constrictor at its lunatic leisure

reminiscent of Riverview, the El, or even the
Polo Grounds and earlier stadia,

all wood, nails and screws,
latticed gridwork and primitive buttresses,

its superstructure the crack of
a bullwhip, the wave

of a virtual lariat. Not too unGuggenheimlike,
either. Painted white—site specific,

I guess. We ride it, burritos
engorge our esophagi, my balls, in the throes

of a series of too sudden de- and then re-escalations, vibrate and rise not
unpleasantly, then we climb out and stagger for root

beer at A Stand Without A Name, saving the Shock Wave for last, woozy
but still on the lookout for saucy

tan kneecaps, that profile . . . In the meantime The Amazing
Alfredeux guesses weights, ages, months of birth and gives special prizes.

At the Moosejaw Trading Post can be purchased genuine woodcraft items,
wind chimes, pottery, no moosejaws at all but still most of the items

you'd expect to discover an An Old-Time Trading Post, while The Plush Pony's
a menagerie, of course, of the latest soft and cuddly stuffed animals . . .

Unearthing the Shock Wave, what will archaeologists make
of two thousand six hundred feet of steel track

with charred, bubbled chips of Dodger blue paint nuked into neat, twisted
loops—some sort of super short, unrapid

transit system for narrow (solar?) cars apparently not
going anyplace terrifically

interesting? These days it slowly climbs 170 feet
up a very steep track, jerkily, nervewracking, clackety *shit*

now there's no turning back as it silently screams into a twelve-story dive
    at 62 m.p.h.
then banks immediately into the first of *you're going to retch*

of the seven, count 'em, inside
out loops inside

of which it *really* starts to jerk you around: upside down,
backward, G-forces whipping you sideways. You turn maybe fifteen

degrees to glance at your son and a twist snaps your head back around.
Your elbow gets banged. You feel giddy and scared, and you understand

clearly that you're going to vomit . . .
The Shock Wave is Great

America's intensest roller-coaster. It is not
a close call. When it stops

and the smiling attendant unlocks your safety *fun?*
bar, you climb out but can't hardly walk. Your kids, of course, both can

and do, way ahead. You, eventually, manage. To, sort of, walk. To see, in
    the unruly lines hurriedly doubling
back for more, that other folks, too, look shook, glazed and happy. They're
    ready.

CAROLYN KOO

WAYS TO DISAPPEAR

I.

Parts of me
scatter into past
tense rooms.

Someone stands
on my hands in the garden,
a gaudy beauty in the drought.
My heart is immobile
in the lap
of a parlor.
My weighted brain
keeps propped
the swinging door.

II.

Swallowed by the monastery.

The brothers tell me
    with their plain eyes,
the walls are bone, the ceiling
stretched, unidentified.

We eat from thin dishes
that curve like shells, and

retire early to nearly
vertical rooms,
chair,
bed,
table-
lamp,

to pray.

III.

Draped in stolen clothes,
I commit a hundred
other tiny crimes.

The weight of kinder words
in a drugged slumber
under my chameleon coat.

Finding incidental parades,
I wave at strangers,
in taffeta, with a wand,
lending meanings
that were never mine.

POWER FAILURE

Waiting is a deliberate
burn tearing at the nerve.
Smoke is still rising from me.
The romance of stilled factories
and cast of incandescent light
coiling like fever into cold.

I can barely delight in the dark
pavement, the tone of a scream
pouring into the snow, the dull
drama and clean angles
of a guest room. Textural medals
of the missing hang with a
greenish patina from the bedposts.

The intellectuals are sad
and can say it in Latin,
pushing away the simple motion
of a palm, hauling their eyes
behind them with twine.
Stitched up, salved over, the
balm soaks through the bandage.

Spit dissolves the light here.
It jerks a moment first,
like the spark of split wire
of the shock
of the recently dead.
Warm birds fall
to a fault in the memory,

the unnatural pitch of a water
tower or tree. Cats and thieves
lean on the soft
moonless lawn, waving
with nocturnal confidence
through clots of curling steam.

MUSIC

I.

The sound of settling
dirt and moving water
through thick infant skin.
Anything but dead to it,
the dissonance is twisting,
   vaguely pleasant
if every other moment is
   a sweetening third.
It stops if you don't listen.

I make shameless
use of it, singing
so it's plain;
happy in the bare
stairwell or naturally,
the bathroom.

   The ache of major seventh,
a constant failure
into flat and sad where
things occur
   in eights.
The natural
   family laughs
at my pathetic arpeggios,
but math
isn't the half of it.

In the blackening caverns
of symphony halls
   I'm leaning
to be moved;
   something we do together
   Taking the bridge like a battle,
we work without tools
forks or flanges.

A shrill manipulation
when the heroine approaches
   the knife,
sweeping as she kisses
the clay of her homeland.
Nicer near windows,
or outside,
traveling only so far.
   The strings are sweating!
The brass cowers in back
while dancers
learn to crack the many
fine bones of the toes.

II.

The way you can't
sleep in the quiet,
the highway,
   the cows.
A slight hunger
of boredom or warmth,
   a sinister whine
in the prop room
full of silver shoes
that lilts the heart
more than a show.

      The teacher will tap
     her lap like a horse
     at first; the imagined
       interval and two-handed
       twang the drop
       into a choppy part B.
     The metronome
       recalls Poe,
     a man's cut
     and bleeding shirt,
     a darkening white.
     It goes this slow
     way for weeks,
     when the room

        is hot
     through the thin
     curtain and someone
     is screaming outside.

An adolescent mystery,
a progression of "ahs" or "uhs"
echoing thickly off the pool tile
where girls under glass
have a sun to judge by.
A three quarter time tale
of glamorous death
   paralyzes the divers
who don't want to be
   flat-chested earth angels,
disembodied heads cradled
by survivors in the dark

        It's mostly at night,
     without license,
     in the park, in the nature
        of a tone,
     falling off the roof
     of a church, a cat
     following the smoke of a plane.
     The places the sane
     store their fingers, a diary
     of desire, as though
     you couldn't stand words
        for a while.

The tired and pleasing
disease of the old,
what they hear
slamming in their skulls,
a plea of memory,
the kiss of an ancient
Agnes or Abigail,
a pause.

        The dry chain
     of an abandoned swing
     in a storm,

the angles
of your face in the sensual
sleep of the greedy.
The rest
   of your shoulders
and smoking low
end of your range,
potent
   and illicit
acoustic
control.

Fruit simply
   rolls to the curb,
   a passerby's rumbling
   percussion to your
practicing through the
muting screen.

III.

The river has a memory
for melody,
its water is suspicious,
unassuming forms like
a low end ghost.
It spits a mimic of desire
back into the thick
air, the breath
of the dead.

The limping hands
   of a broken watch,
I court silence
   with fists full
of the terrible past;
with sleeping
   near the theater
at the feet
of crowd scene dancers.

The peculiar
misery of a city,
   its bruises,
    eyes
    and waiting
for the shadow
to fall behind you,
robbed of a moment's notice.

I hold the ladder
for shirtless workers,
   their charm
and pretended ineptness
as they grip
   each other's wrists,
dancing on the scaffold.
They linger after parties,
   converse
in the sticky kitchen,
confessing affection
   while their hands
rest in the ice.

Everyone knows the words.

The piano has a faint,
   even pulse;
blood looks
   good on it.
I cover my clean eyes
and seem
to slip
   through a cut
in the quiet
lining of a sea.

ANGELA GOODRICH

PIANO CIRCLES

Triangles of light
wind worn

Resting on my old oak floor
space in sudden
clouds to storm
not here

Where icicles drip trumpets
into the afternoon and
pale winter washes
in the small curve of
childish waves

Bright balance dancing in bare feet
under the sap smell
of inside places

KEVIN CASSIDY

READING

I know how the senses trail off. I feel them
deepen and drift. The book I was reading
drops to the floor like a child who wakes in the night.
A woman walking on the page keeps walking.
A dusty road in the west. She has three cigarettes,
a man's shirt, a bundle of notes she has written:
Time is not a line or a circle but several things in layers.

The paper is moist from the breath of trees
and the letters are shaped like branches
still living though everything has changed.
The way the water moves and the perfect blue
of the sky are called by another name.
The woman knows more than she can say
and she says there is more than she knows.

Clouds gather while the small town sleeps
and crows have flown over her head.
It could be the crows are my own two eyes
moving beneath the dark. It could be I'm dreaming,
the sleeping body passed hand over hand through the carbon,
through darkness that carries me breathing and whole
through the clay that shifts in the ground.

SUPPLICANT

By and by the house will collapse
and every tooth will fall from my head

The birds will build nests where I keep my cups
and the mice will make beds of my books

A laughing child twirls in circles
just outside the house and I am helpless

Everywhere the melting snow
blackens the greening ground

I fear I will cease to be human,
that my body will feather its edges

my body will disperse in the light
that keeps on gathering toward me

I should just kneel on the stones
and place my palms on the ground

I should sink like water and seek
the way that runs into the river

I could push into the swiftest current
where it glides by my widening eyes

and each person I pass could become
someone I would touch and tell my name

A STUDY OF VERMEER

Light has become like a word in my mind
like a room that welcomes the senses.
A woman holding pearls by the window
or a woman pouring milk in a bowl, a balance
held in a woman's hands, a piece of paper
glowing in her fingers as if it were light itself.

The light pouring in upon the body, softening the skin,
her silent attention inventing solitude,
each object fixed in the feminine pull,
the presence in each vessel of the one not seen.
The world's wide air mingling in the breath,
in the moist rose that closes as day turns into night.

The way the light is constant, transforming itself
entirely into shadow, the way the body would empty,
the ache to go where the light has gone
across the face of creation. The wish to be
as shadows are, dense and self-possessed,
falling, incessantly widening in the real.

By my own window it is not so quiet.
Apple blossoms blow through the air
as the apple tree comes apart.
Cock-shape maple seeds wing down
and stand themselves in the grassblades.
Green shoots come through every crack.
No moment can stay, here, where I am.

MARIA CARLOTA NELSON

NOTES ON A DISILLUSIONED SPANISH COUPLE
VISITING MOSCOW

I'm sitting in room 1507.
I've learned how to make
this dark room mine by
naming all the splattered
mosquitos on the wall . . . I've
given them names: Jose, Rocio.
Margarita is the fat one near
the lampshade.
The floor is cold, it's been
a busy day, I feel dreams leaking
in from other rooms, windows, the
many tourists slurring in their sleep,
the taste of foreign coins in their
mouths. I know they are still trying
to accustom themselves to the heat and
murmurs in a different language,
sounds they will never learn.
A taste they will never want to acquire:
cabbage soup, slippery goat cheese,
warm green soda.
Poor Doña Agustina, she came to me with
a broken face, tears welling up, hiding
in her ears: "We cannot go to sleep,"
she tells me, "my husband is crying . . .
what will we tell our grandchildren
of Russia?" I opened my arms but
she did not want them. She slapped me,
her aged trembling hand on my
face like a disappointed mother.
"I'm sorry," I said, understanding.
"Come, I will sing you a song."
I put her husband to sleep, whispering
in his ears a ballad from his country:
"Asturias . . . Patria querida . . ." He
fell asleep on Agustina's breast. She

kissed my temple, now warm.
Only four more days, I thought as I
walked up to my room. They'll go
back and they'll go silent, saying
nothing about the great motherland.
Franco's books will no longer be
dusted or studied, Stalin's pictures
will be taken down from their icon-walls
full of 15th century crosses from Burgos.
Half their lives dreaming of stepping on
these fields and roads "made for everyone,
where everything is for everyone . . ."
There is more to it, Doña Agustina:
Everything is for everyone . . . but here
there is nothing to share.

RUARI FENNESSY

BEAUTY, YOU'RE AN UGLY THING

The beauty of it all is that
    there was no beauty.
  Sure, you had the surf,
the sixth sunrise and waterfall
    you never washed yourself in.
  You had the chorus of swallows
  and the dolphins whisper, even
the rainbows in the "imagine yourself
there" park even had it a little.

IT. What a cursed word.
  But I say it again:
The beauty of it all was that there was
        no beauty.

    The crystal sleeping in a dark earth
    that only shines after you dig it
  up and hold it to some bragging light.

    The crystal never knowing this destiny
    of being the beauty of it all.

EDWARD MOORE

NOVEMBER

I long to be a
true manchild with
a head on his
shoulders, with a
serious mind for
serious things

deepened to frenzy
by nights ridden
along creeping
stream water and
gnarled boughs
backlit by

quarter-moonlight
briefly. The air
seems frequent
and moved: leaves
hooved into the
moist without

noting the scent
of gore in the
mud, of dead
fingers grasping,
holding near on
such formal flesh.

THE SEAMS

Time spent sniffling
the turpentine years,
the slipslide hours of
grace and aptitude that

rattle the ends, that
set off the winky little
in-jokes about moving

through this vast
velvet space with
coffee breath and
no urge to find

God, don't get
tacked on the way
knotted shoelace days

waiting to be greased
and relieved do. The
corners hold gently, but
the in-between crumbles

like Jimmy Cagney
tight-fisted screaming
"Top of the world, Ma!

Top of the world!" And
this doesn't settle a
thing. Too bad the nights
are so real, so bolted:

Horns seen by streetlight
that have never been fingered;
boomerang moon dipping

behind a cloud to run
the Hail Mary Pattern;
cups filling and dropping
over like smiles at

a wedding. There are
worries about how tight
the stitching should be,

about working on pages
for an untitled breakdown
whose meanings are
turtled by too much

study, by never coming
to terms with broken
July or the ashes of

heartbeaten weekends. But
things still make their
presence known, creeping
desperation into the

fever dream, making
it all whipped-puppy
wasted. Knowledge of

"Making the Juicy," of
lacing words together for
impression's sake isn't
demanded here like knowing

that "Yes" and "Yes"
are opposites when one
means maybe or that

open-ended curiosity is
fatal are. But being
dead is the easy trip:
Don't have to thirst

after smooth minutes
to fold in tiny squares
and tuck behind my

Master Card and favorite
poet—don't have to decide

how many women won't
be spoken to today.

Baseball cards mark
the chapters like
dividers in a magician's

trick, but the studies
slog on, making me
scoop air with my
tongue for the sake

of heaving, making me
settle on the floor and
tear myself to sleep.

CYNTHIA TODD CAPPELLO

CARRIED AWAY

The board-bare platform scrapes horizon
where two tracks turn to one.
I hear the whistle and clutch
my ticket, tight as a preacher's smile,
between finger and thumb.
It's coming;
the glint of diesel, puffing lush
its message along the rails,
gleaming its sleek trip down the track.
Coming for me.

I want to ride the Orient Express
with you, to start, not here,
but Paris
after nights in gold and black cafés
or walks along the river seeking
old earth-scented books
in languages we'd like to learn.
After you buy a caricature of me
drawn by a stranger
and feed me soft grey cheese
on crusty bread with bottled water,
we'll board.

We'll board our private coach
named for some goddess of antiquity.
The polished marquetry will glow with
flower and fruit for us.
We'll sup brocaded, crystalized, and
watch the countryside slide by;
we'll dine
on salmon, caviar and oysters,
tiny sugar cubes
and tulip shadows cast by fixtures
overhead.

Then, closeted, we'll love
on high-count linen and let
the rhythm, the rhythm
lull us until the porter morning.

We'll disembark in Istanbul
to dance and play sweet, wild
musical instruments
and stuff ourselves with figs,
to wrap the spiced wool
of a foreign country around us
until we sweat,
then, shoulders aching,
turn
and start the journey home.

THE LONG END OF SEPTEMBER

I came to Cannes end of season
and by accident
walked the midnight length of the harbor
in tight black tourist shoes.
You held my hand.

On our right were anchored
a hundred ships we'd never pilot
along the Cote d'Azur.
I read their names aloud.

Opposite the shops were closed.
The one open café set silhouettes
of black and gold against the night.
What laughter there was
echoed.

You pointed out the sacred place
of silver fantasy,
deserted now,
the audience and critics gone,
the massive doors shut tight.

Tonight we lie
not far from Grasse
behind lace-curtained windows
shuttered against the starlight.
In your sleep you toss and mumble.

When I'm gone
you will no longer dream in English.

JULIE DIANE SPEARS

RED

The cranberry glass goblet
stood on the
shelf
for seven years
and the chairs
sprayed white
echoed red vibrations
underneath it all
Stop
the red light
blinking red
The heartbeat
underneath it all
said Stop

I was crying and It I couldn't stop Tears Staining Tears Streaking I was in
love was in love with Tears are streaking and I walked in on two bodies in
my bed two bodies No tears but I was crying Tears Streaking She left the
room Streaking I was shaking Crying I turned and left the room Crying

Her hands were
ragged and frayed
like ancient lace dust rags
She placed her hand
on my knee and laughed
It didn't echo
was hollow and empty
Shaking off the tension and the shaking
of her own hand
It'll pass, she said,
It'll pass

SUNG KOO

THE THREE WORDS ONE

The secrets dissipate
against your will
and you're stereotyped
in a roomful
of slack-jawed gazers.
The sullen tweed
of your smile
reveals your complacency.
Yet, you segue
into a sashay
of dime-store memories.
You hope for
a moment's notice
and a bigot
who takes advantage
of celluloid ambiguity.
You bite yourself
into a stillness
created by Nostradamus
and swim back
to yesterday's prediction
to find obituaries
scattered and frayed
by gutless fiction.
Born-again gossipers say
that you're growing
fat on the
final, bottom line.

THE COMPETITION

It is the constant jungle
  that runs beside you
and solidifies you
  in a graceful moment.
Even the gazelles are jealous
  of your agile consonants.
If what the larger predators
  say is true,
then you are safer than
  the suicidal pendulums
of an urban majority.

I know of your longing
  to find yourself
in a favorite movie
  where you are fed straight lines.
But for the moment,
  you are a World War II newsreel,
and the Nazis want
  your boyish haircut.

SONNET FOR KAFKA'S FAMILY

The pensive piano shudders under my calloused fingertips;
and for the moment, chromatic is a breezy metaphor for noise.
A car drags its muffler, and the romantic balladeer inside me
justifies this as rhythm. I whirl with ease. I am filled with
religious bourbon and the power to admit my shortcomings freely
with strangers, bankers, back-up singers, and daft runaways.
This is piss ecstasy! The whole reason why algebra corresponds so well
with my thighs. I once heard someone say that I was an approaching
carnival. Insult or not, this could be my funeral dress, or worse,
my orphan ego. On sombre days, I have misread this to be pure
shivers. It is the fate of the optimistic ichthyologist, like myself,
who spits half-heartedly at his or her inferiors. I could easily towel
dry these nocuous mumblings and package it into the realm
of forgotten health classes. On better days, my friends call me Chuck.

JOHN BOYER

DUSK

(for H. D. Boyer)

We stood so the day slanted,
unequal sunlight on our shoulders.
The idea was for a gentle
ending like a cool pillow on
the face at night
and an arm
laid across the chest.
Our last grass-chewing story
then off the fence post and the
walk back the chalk-wet gravel.
A round sort of time that
comes back on a Sunday dusk
in a lawn chair
after he's gone and
I can smell him
in the sunset.

STABBED

It is the edge so thin to push
flesh in either direction that
I am afraid of.
A cut to show me inside,
the taken for granted question
a dying man told me,
blood,
or just that it is possible
everything inside me might come out.
My fingers stick against each other;
dreams, knowledge
and memories
puddle together on the tile.
A good long gash may show
nothing like the ice pick
that drills into the chest, left hanging
like a forgotten syringe.
This inquisitive gesture,
this suicide from a stranger
will let the last drop to
roll down the arm be the answer,
or the first drop never be seen.

SCHOOCHER'S LADDERS

Sometimes she calls me chance as
we sit naked, spitting bourbon
through our teeth on the rug.
She talks about bowling and
asks if I've had the same
trouble with my hook.
It's then, Bacos in hand,
that I can see why I'm there
and would give it all
to hold her.

KATHLEEN DUNNE

SEASON OF KNIVES

Ceilings are high
and heat climbs out of reach.
I get edgy up to my elbows
in the evening's dishes.

Men cannot bear to be alone,
I fume. Or oneness:
reading four books at once,
shuffling the tracks of
ten albums,
flipping channels all night.

The good knives drying right,
lethal side up.

He threw them in the sink
just any old way. As if
I counted knives that cut the meal,
marking where they fell.
I hiss "Russian Roulette,
the Lousy Scout."

On cue, a point draws blood,
black under a nail.
Tears come in no proportion to pain.

Just wipe the skillet clean,
he said. Soap pits the iron.
I want to scour the thing
clean as spite.

The water running right,
hot as I can stand it.

MICHAEL CRONIN

"I WAS TALKING ABOUT . . ."

I was talking about
the last few parts
of me
left
without a trace of you
traded with a drop
of water
inside
I was thinking of trees
made striped glistening stone
by time,
by water,
pieces moved one at a time
with a metronome beat
you for me,
you for me,
infused color banding
along me
in frozen fissures
I have revealed,
and I feel
you for me—
I was wondering
why living stone
is warm
to the touch

MARGARET SZCZERBINSKI

JAN. 1, 1992

Let's walk it's such great exercise
Her melon rind lips squeezed
the first hollows of jealousy
The music of her people
sang around her in tempo
I was not aware of the notes
only lust of a passing stranger
An antique watch with a bent chain
made me dizzy for a chase
I lost two dollars
while leaning over a bridge
Made three wishes for the New Year
Some Frenchman smelled of mint
pressed his hand on my cheek
which made my friend laugh
A bookstore in an alley
Cobblestone gold beneath urban trash
Wood and print tempt my treasure chest
But what got me was the aristocrat
in the red-buttoned coat.

ELIZABETH HERRON

DESERT ROSE

Night after night the dizzying sky
swims with stars
sanded bright by the wind.
Sunrise comes fast and hot
and welcome because the nights
are cold, even in August.

He's still asleep, so I find what I need
to make coffee, then sit on the doorstep,
put aside my memories and my plans
and let the sun eat me up.

Inside the trailer, light needles its way
through tiny holes in the blind.
He groans and his eyelids flutter.
I watch his face while I slide
his keys and cash off the dresser.

I start the pick-up. When I pull out
I hear the gravel shoot away
from the tires, and something else—
his voice maybe, but I don't look back.

I drive toward town, shadows
to the west of fence posts,
pools of shade ahead of each tumbleweed,
the truck's twin running beside me on the dirt,
nearer town, the new black asphalt.

I park and get out. By now it's bright,
so I put on dark glasses. Sun
glares off the sidewalk, the cars,
the sides of buildings.
At the drugstore I stop and look in
the window. I pretend I'm looking
at the display, but I'm looking at myself.

Behind me the state police cruise
around the corner, the trooper's head
swivels toward me as he drifts by
in the patrol car. I pretend not to notice,
turn away from the window and walk
toward the casino.

The desert light flattens things
like they've been smoothed out
on an ironing board. People look
two-dimensional, buildings
like sets. I'm walking in somebody's
movie. I can feel the trooper still
watching me. I walk faster.

I'm walking east. Even with my glasses,
it's blinding. At the corner I start to run.
My legs are heavy and my head spins,
but I keep running. I hear the car
turn after me, but I don't stop.
I run straight toward the sun,
into the empty light.

JACKIE MONAHAN

CABIN FEVER

Spacious rooms are not meant
to be mine.
I must write
in my closet's maze,
tube of toothpaste
in my path.
Hurricane child
rearranging my thoughts
while I'm away.
I have given up the notion
of being deep,
settling instead
for deceptively shallow,
unlikely geisha
figure-flawed, ruddy,
cleaning my paper houses
with darkest ink
like opening a vein
of my own (so)
that others might
(softly)
be created.

SERAFINA CHAMBERLIN

WRITERS AT YELLOW BAY

The last night in Montana
I dream of deep, cold lakes
Of unending blue
Broken-free winged carousel horses
Fly by
Peaceful waking
Head filled with everything said
Read
Written—
At breakfast Ana says, "I had such wonderful
    dreams last night!"
Sly glance at the silver and onyx
Bracelet on her wrist
I laugh and say, "So did I"
Hold up my own intricate sterling filigree
Bought from a quiet-voiced poet
Who tells me of his own journey from the Midwest
How he found his way
    to this imaginary place for good
And ever
Writes in his book
"I hope the poems open up for you"—
I smile at Ana
"You think Lowell did it, don't you?"
We laugh together—
Chicago sunset landing
Sleep
    only to hear the St. Ignatius
Mission bell
    beckon from the mountains
Clear, in the dark.

BRIAN RAY

THE FARTHER

I have not arrived
somehow I feel there anyway
under new moons
and willow trees
past ancient windows
with stained-glass tears
and farther
past the hands of my grandfather
wound round new hats
sweating in steam and wood
and concrete walls
and still I am farther
beyond the curb
where my father's blood
ran over broken vodka bottles
and still I am farther
past the fallen oak
beyond the beam
on wooden legs
like thunder walking
alone with my majik
and the heartbeat of God
still I am farther
closer to the blackened hole
of dreams stolen like
whispers from the dying
still I am farther
onward to the desolate
beauty of my forever

FRANK CORPUS

GREEN NOIR

Black lights lifting up trees
in frenzied waves of repulsion
where no one knows
the resembling detachments of sulfur and shade.

Before the windows stand marble slabs
that crack in their own misery.
These windows look out onto the forest
but never show the x-rays of nature.

To stand alone beyond woods of the obscene
so that no one can say how lonely you are
when you spend an eternity painting shadows in color.

And only when you come back to reason
there comes more notice to enthrall the faces that
peek from umbrellas in a storm of
black colors and dim light.

And to this all
and all this too
like falling from evil
at the end of a sermon.

Or being forgotten
in the trees and weeds
left paling in the fog
and burning for reason.

MAUREEN McINERNY

YOU ROLL OVER

You roll over like the collar of my shirt, with purpose but no form. Loving the high spot on the floor where the door always catches (and that gritty sound). You roll over like waves, leaving me to wake up with fingertips feeling left out, after dreaming that we had done it. You roll over me like a cotton swab sucking its meal with intent. Throwing your head back as if someone was on top of you, on top of me. The knowing of this rolling, continuous and dedicated, has caused me to roll also. And in such a small white room, we will surely be lost, or watched at least. Like two seahorses who move too slow to fight, but love and eat nonetheless.

JOSEPH RAMIREZ

AIRVÁTA

Convection
Confetti
a tumbling center pulls upward
and you become an
          inhaler of scapes.

Ridgetops look backwards
and wooden profiles jettison
in your heaving lungs

Before me thickets of yellow stalks,
shafts of weathered wood.
The gate opens by gusts
and I am rushed through
to blues
to transparent scents
          like ginger roots.

You awakened to fluid mountains,
chatoyant one, and lived in
                    lakes of air.
And while your wings were seared
by iridescent will,

I curled like a dog to induce dreams
to watch stars sewn, blown,
                    under your skin.

These were tucked in white wetness
under your eyes
behind your thighs
into your belly
into your ears—the sound
of iron struck—all slit then tucked.

An embryo elephant,
still smaller than my face,
floating in fat and flesh
for twenty-two months, you
          breathed the upper world.

Then your padded womb-bed bled
                         spilled,
and you rolled out
like particles of light
               diverging downstairs
like wet lead ladled out
          from warm air
          to cold air.

The hemispheres slow
   and you are caught moving
like abalone move.

WILLIAM PAUL HICKEY

THE AMAZING DISAPPEARING PILOT

So roll away the
impermanence of
your face.

They're paving
the ocean to
let you
rollerskate
to Europe where
fish is the
only currency
(so tenderly legal)

I can see them
drawing chalk
outlines
for the dead
airmen and
drowned
sailors.

The asphalt
now
a deeper green,

flecked with
purple so

I stop to buy
licorice
scented candles

to light in the
cellophane grotto
for Amelia,
the amazing disappearing
pilot

HEATHER DILLON

DYING YOUNG

I take my hands and run them across
my baldness,
the hills and grooves
worn smooth like a pebble washed
clean in the ocean,
the scars I couldn't see when they hid
in hair
raising beneath my fingertips
I rub the softened surface
caging
a jelloed skull
and feel my brain beat.

It's not as if I can't touch you
anymore because I don't have
hair—
I don't want to anymore.
The icy water rises and falls
and beats against
the rocks
rushing in,
swallowing us like a whale
who spits you out and
leaves me sitting inside his mouth,
a bald Jonah
with frozen nervetips
and a brain that forever beats
thump-thump, thump-thump.

Oh, give a little—what do I have
left to give
my hair? The strands of thread that
hid my screaming thoughts, that
blanketed them like fog over the ocean
that covered me
from death and
your eyes.

KAREN LONG

ROOMS

stand here.
can you
feel her?
she watches.
those footsteps,
my rapid heartbeat,
hear it.
hands tremble
for no reason,
just habit.
this room
is her eyes.
and in corners
our shadows
battle
while here
in the middle
she smiles
but oh,
in corners
of rooms,
of my eyes.
there is no refuge,
not one
unbloodied
place.
so i wander
and shake,
jump
at my father's
rumble.
he is
puzzled,
and i cannot
explain.
the walls

are screaming,
so high
only i
can hear it
squealing
inside
my head.
how could
i tell him
that if i
am alone
in my room
and hear
footsteps
i try
to hide.
even
from him.
i forget
that i am
not a child.
it is
because
the eyes
always,
her eyes
in this room
i tremble
and try
to hide
crouched
in a corner
and always
opposite,
over the bed
around a chair
she advances
twisted red
her anger
rushing
at me like
a shock wave
wall of air

in front.
and when
i am alone
in the whole
quiet house
i stand
at the long
mirror
my head
twisted round
looking at
rivers of
broken blood
mapped in
strange
red purple
patterns
against my
white,
white skin,
back and butt
and thighs.
i touch
them, ever
so gently,
marveling
at the soft
pain.